To

_____

From

_____

Date

_____

21 Days

Prayer Power for a

Great
Turnaround

Dr. James O. Fadel

21 Days Prayer Power for a Great Turnaround

Published by

Fadel Publishing International
515 County Road 1118
Greenville, TX 75401
www.jamesfadel.com

Cover & Layout Design by

Cornerstone Creativity Group LLC
Phone: +1(516) 547-4999
info@thecornerstonepublishers.com
www.thecornerstonepublishers.com

Printed in the United States of America.

CONTENTS

Introduction

THE GREAT TURNAROUND

"The ark of God remained with the family of Obed-Edom in his house three months. And the LORD blessed the house of Obed-Edom and all that he had." (1 Chronicles 13:14)

I welcome you to the year 2020, the year of the Great Turnaround. In discussing a Great Turnaround, it is necessary that we define the component terms. The word "great" is often used for an important or distinguished person; it also means enormous, colossal, extreme, jumbo, stupendous, excellent or glorious. "Turnaround" is a combination of two words, "turn" and "around". To turn is to change position, to reverse position or placement, to shift or twist or change from one state to another. "Around" means all sides, or all over, or throughout.

Put together, a Great Turnaround means that God, the excellent, glorious and distinguished Person in this equation, will move or cause you to change on all sides. It means that God will reverse the irreversible concerning you. That which you have lost, and you think is gone, God will bring it back. When God turns to you, it is your turn; your story will change from good to better and from better to best.

In 1 Chronicles 13:14, quoted above, we are concisely told the story of Obed-Edom's transformation; his great turnaround from nobody to somebody. Here are a few other examples of divine turnarounds in the Bible:

Abram: Figuratively, he could not afford the rent in a different house, so he was hanging around his parents, though married, until God called him, and he obeyed. By the time we read of him again in Genesis 13:2, we are told, *"...Abram was very rich in cattle, in silver, and in gold."* God, indeed, continued to bless him mightily. Genesis 14:19 says, *"And He blessed him, and said, blessed be Abram of the most high God, possessor of heaven and earth."*

Jephthah: He was a bastard (Judges 11:1,3) that became a Prime Minister. He had been sent packing from his father's house before God intervened and gave him a great turnaround. *"And the elders of Gilead said unto Jephthah, Therefore we turn again to thee now, that thou mayest go with us, and fight against the children of Ammon, and be our head over all the inhabitants of Gilead."* (Judges 11:8)

A robber that was crucified with Jesus: Two robbers were crucified on each side of Jesus. One was hard-hearted and mocked Jesus while the other repented. The repentant robber seeing that Jesus was innocent and believing that He was the Son of God, asked Jesus to remember him when He came into His Kingdom. Jesus promised they would be together that very day in Paradise (Luke 23:39-43).

Saul: One who was a religious fanatic and persecutor of "The People of The Way" - disciples and members of the body of Christ (Acts 9:1-2). He was transformed. No longer a terrorist, his heart became filled with the love of Jesus and love for God's people (Philippians 1:8, 2:1-2; 1 Thessalonians 2:7-8).

These and many others are pointers to what God can do and will do in your life as you wholeheartedly embark on this prayer exploit.

PRAYER POINTS

Begin by declaring the following prayer points:

1. Father, I thank you for you alone are God. I exalt and appreciate you for 2019 and 2020. Thank you that I didn't go with 2019. Thank you for bringing me thus far. LORD, accept my thanks, worship and adoration.

2. Blood of Jesus, cleanse me totally from every defilement of the spirit, soul and body and from every pride, self-will, and pomposity. I know full well that empty barrels make the most noise. Please, LORD, cleanse me of every sin that is yet to be forgiven me right now, in Jesus' name.

3. Every implantation and establishment of Satan in my life and destiny, I command you to be uprooted by the divine wind of change, in Jesus' name.

4. Every demonic wall and barrier that is standing between me and God, collapse now by fire, in Jesus' name.

5. I receive an attitude of thanksgiving, as well as the grace to examine myself and remain teachable every day of the year 2020, in Jesus' mighty name.

6. Oh God, open unto me the door of your power and abilities, doors of your treasures and blessings, doors of your secrets and mysteries from today, in Jesus' name.

7. Father, let the rain of your blessings fall consistently on me, in Jesus' name. Please, let your Presence go ahead of me in this new year, in Jesus' name. Anointing for fruitfulness and plenty in all areas of life, fall on me today, in Jesus' name.

8. Father, I receive a great turnaround now in my life, family, church, community, state and country, in the mighty name of Jesus.

Thank God for answered prayers.

Day 1

HEAVEN ON EARTH

"That your days may be multiplied, and the days of your children, in the land which the LORD sware unto your fathers to give them, as the days of heaven upon the earth."
(Deuteronomy 11:21)

In the key text quoted above, the LORD looked at the children of Israel and desired to give them a taste of heaven on earth. The same is true of His intent towards us, His children, even today. God wants to give us a taste of heaven on earth. While everyone has an idea and a viewpoint, I believe God has spoken without stuttering. There are two answers to every question: God's answer and everyone else's; and everyone else is wrong! So, I encourage you to bow to God's answer on this issue of heaven on earth – believe it, live it and enjoy the blessing!

- You can experience heaven on earth in your personal life (3 John 2). You can experience heaven on earth in your family (1 Samuel 25:6).

- You can experience heaven on earth in your church (Matthew 16:16-19)

- You can experience heaven on earth in your community (Isaiah 62:12).

As regards experiencing the days of heaven on earth, this is what God has promised, and this promise will be yours, in Jesus' name.

PRAYER POINTS

1. Worship the Creator of the heaven and the earth. Bless Jehovah El-Shaddai, the LORD of Lords, the King of Kings, the Monarch of the Universe. Daniel 4:3 says, *"How great are His signs! and how mighty are His wonders! His kingdom is an everlasting kingdom, and His dominion is from generation to generation."*

2. Psalms 8:4-5 says, *"What is man that Thou art mindful of him, and the son of man, that Thou visitest him? For Thou has made him a little lower than the angels and crowned him with glory and honor."* God's desire is for you to be covered with glory and honor. Shame and dishonor are never part of His plan for you. Pray that every manifestation of shame and dishonor in your life should come to an end today, in Jesus' name.

Now, make these declarations:

3. I command the spirit of "Esek" (contention) and the spirit of "Sitnah" (opposition) assigned against my inheritance to die by fire, in Jesus' name. (Genesis 26:20-22).

4. It is written in Deuteronomy 32:13, *"He made him ride on the high places of the earth, that he might eat the increase of*

the fields; and he made him to suck honey out of the rock, and oil out of the flinty rock." Father, let me ride on the high places of the earth, enjoying the best of life. What is hard for others shall be easy for me, in Jesus' name.

5. Father, create in me a thirst and hunger for the return of the LORD Jesus; a deep longing for a fresh revelation of the soon-coming King. Help me to place an intimate relationship with you above making requests of you, in Jesus' name!

6. Deliver me, O LORD, from lukewarm or forced obedience. I know a servant can serve without love. Father make me to love you and everything that pertains to you. I give myself away so I can love you more.I am exempted from plagues, in Jesus' name. I'm not a candidate for evil. I'm not a victim of evil association. My journey to greatness will not be terminated at a bus stop of life, as it happened to Terah, in Jesus' name.

Thank you, LORD, for answered prayers — MARANATHA!

Day 2

GOD HAS REMEMBERED ME

"And God remembered Rachel, and God hearkened to her, and opened her womb. And she conceived, and bare a son; and said, God hath taken away my reproach." (Genesis 30:22-23)

I want this declaration to sink deep into your soul and heart, until it becomes your heartbeat. Let it fill every fiber of your being. Let it course through your bloodstream till it becomes your very life.

The word "remember" is very interesting, no doubt; but there is something before that which I want you to see.

AND GOD…

In Genesis 30:22, the Bible says, *"…And God remembered Rachel and God hearkened to her and opened her womb."* I will modify this expression a bit for emphasis. *"And God remembered Rachel. And God hearkened to her. And God opened her womb."* I like that. "And God, and God, and God". Every time you see the phrase "And God," it means that God is making an entrance into a place or situation and getting involved. Psalms 24:7, for instance, says, *"Lift up your heads, O you gates! And be lifted up, you everlasting doors! And the King of glory shall come in."*

This means that when God remembered Rachel and hearkened unto her, He opened her womb. Now, we may be tempted to think that the use of that word "remember" has to do with God being jolted into action by His memory. But God never ever forgets. In actual fact, that scripture and other scriptures that speak about memories are making a statement about seasons and confirmation of a time. What happened in the case of Rachel, therefore, is that God entered a season that was set for her situation to be turned around and it was.

I decree that God will open something great concerning your life. Every door that the enemy has closed against you shall be opened, in Jesus' name.

PRAYER POINTS

Lift your hands and shout with the voice of triumph. Thank the LORD, bless Him, shout hallelujah and declare your love for Him.

Now declare:

1. O LORD, remember my community and country for good, in the name of Jesus.

2. According to Matthew 16:18, Father, remember your church for good in Jesus' name.

3. O LORD, remember me. Wipe away anything that should not be in my life, in Jesus' name (Matthew 15:13). Remember my labor.

4. Father, bring my reproach to an end. I ask for deliverance. Give me supernatural openings. Fulfil my

desires and longings. Add to your church all through this week, this month and this year, in Jesus' name.

5. I have come into my season. I have come into my programmed time; I have come into my scheduled moment. I decree it like Hannah did. Let the gates be opened. Let the door of my womb be opened. Let the door of prosperity be opened unto me. Let the door of favor be opened. Let the door of ministry be opened. Let the door of increase be opened. Let the door of blessing be opened. Let the door of promotion be opened. Let the door of light be opened. Let every good door be opened for me, in the name of Jesus.

6. I ask, O LORD, because of your grace and mercy, let today mark the end of every judgment against me and my family, in the mighty name of Jesus. The prey of the terrible shall be delivered and the lawful captive shall be set free (Isaiah 49:25). Every error, mistake, sin that the devil is using against me, let today mark the end of it, in the mighty name of Jesus.

7. I decree deliverance for my loved ones: my father, my mother, my spouse and my children. Every yoke in your life is broken, in the name of Jesus.

8. I prophesy the end of my reproach; it is over. Before this week ends, every request I made by God's word is granted, in Jesus' name. My long-awaited expectation is released.

9. I announce, in the name of JESUS, that there shall be no loss. I prophesy revival upon my nation and church, in the name of Jesus.

10. I receive these miracles with a thunderous clap, in Jesus' mighty name.

Day 3

PHAREZ ANOINTING (TO OVERTAKE)

"Now it came to pass, at the time for giving birth, that behold, twins were in her womb. And so it was, when she was giving birth, that the one put out his hand; and the midwife took a scarlet thread and bound it on his hand, saying, "This one came out first." Then it happened, as he drew back his hand, that his brother came out unexpectedly; and she said, "How did you break through? This breach be upon you!" Therefore, his name was called Pharez. Afterward his brother came out who had the scarlet thread on his hand. And his name was called Zerah." (Genesis 38:27-30, NKJV)

Many people who are meant for the top find themselves at the bottom. Many are struggling to maintain the victory they once received. Many fight battles all their lives; as children, they fought; as teenagers, they fought; and now as adults or aged people, they are still fighting.

So, what does it mean to overtake? To overtake is to achieve a level once obtained but lost, in which case, the level lost is not only recaptured but also surpassed, and that even by surprise.

When Pharez exited the womb, the midwife asked, *"How hast thou broken forth?"* From our text, it was time for Tamar to deliver her set of twins and the midwife was ready. One of the two boys, later named Zerah, got the first opportunity for breakthrough. He put his hand out and the midwife joyfully announced, "This came out first," and put a red scarlet around his wrist. This was to recognize the first and supposed head of the leading clan in Judah, the ancestor of David and, ultimately, Christ. But alas, that was not to be. Because, suddenly this boy, Zerah, withdrew back into the womb and, at that very point, the second boy emerged from the womb and came out completely. The midwife amazedly asked, *"How hast thou broken forth (overtaken)?"*

This really was a breakthrough for this boy who was later named Pharez, meaning, "breaking forth". He was to come last, but he came first. "How did you do it?" The midwife asked! As they were "crowning" Pharez the leader, Zerah, who had the first shot at breakthrough, came out and it was a pity. So, Pharez became the head of the leading clan in Judah and, thus, an ancestor of David and ultimately of Christ (Ruth 4:18-22; Matthew 1:1-3).

Now, even though we are talking of babies here, the process and the drama at the birth of this set of twins as one overtook the other has spiritual significance and vital lessons for a break forth.

Although it was determined that there were twins in the womb, there was no scanning machine, and the mother pushing couldn't see anything. She and her children were at the mercy of the midwife, who quickly tagged the first wrist out with a scarlet thread to recognize the elder. However, the unexpected happened when the baby withdrew his hand, and his brother came forth. The dumbfounded midwife could only wonder how he broke forth.

If you have people who are already laughing at you, simply connect to the God of Pharez and you will see what will happen.

Jesus is with you, so His power and ability are also with you. This power will change your position and story. You will operate in violent faith and give the enemy no alternative, telling him that, "I want my position that has been stolen."

PRAYER POINTS

Make the following declarations:

1. Father, in the name of Jesus, I come before you, come into my life, take control of my life, in Jesus' mighty name.

2. Every Judas assigned against my prosperity, perish, in the name of Jesus.

3. Anything in my life stealing my uncommon breakthroughs, clear away, in the name of Jesus.

4. By the power in the blood of Jesus, O God arise and make a way for me where there is no way, in Jesus' name.

5. My reality is defined by the words of Isaiah 55:12 which says, *"For ye shall go out with joy, and be led forth with peace: the mountains and the hills shall break forth before you into singing, and all the trees of the field shall clap their hands."*

6. I command every monitoring spirit following my progress to be blinded forever, in Jesus' name.

7. I am tired of the highway of sorrow, I exit into joy, peace and prosperity, in Jesus' name.

8. I disarm every family strongman fighting against my breakthrough, in Jesus' name.

9. I declare that in life, I will always be at the right place at the right time.

10. I reject accidents on my way to breakthrough, in Jesus' name.

11. I reject setbacks and fruitless labor, in Jesus' name.

12. I recover every lost opportunity, in Jesus' name.

13. From now on, I shall excel in all I do, in Jesus' name.

Day 4

A GREAT HARVEST OF BLESSING

"Say not ye, there are yet four months, and then cometh harvest? behold, I say unto you, lift up your eyes, and look on the fields; for they are white already to harvest. I sent you to reap that whereon ye bestowed no labor: other men labored, and ye are entered into their labors." (John 4:35,38)

This day promises abundant life, unlimited riches and hidden treasures in Christ for you. It is your special privilege to plunge into God's inexhaustible storehouse and receive until your joy is full. God is prepared to bless, and you must be prepared to receive too. *"...be abundantly satisfied with the fatness of [His] house; and drink of the river of [His] pleasures."* (Psalm 36:8, paraphrase mine).

Where the harvest is concerned, it is wise for you to: (i.) set goals (ii.) secure necessary permissions (iii.) sanctify [set apart] yourself (iv.) support God's work with prayer and finance (v.) seek to get the best (vi.) serve with commitment and dedication, and (vii.) spread the new of God's goodness and faithfulness abroad.

"While the earth remaineth, seedtime (not seed-season) *and harvest* (timing and quantity determined by God)..., *shall not cease"* (Genesis 8:22). Proper seed planted in proper ground under proper conditions, always produces a

proper harvest.

What is harvest? Harvest can be a gathering in of crops; a time of the year when mature grains, fruit, vegetables, etc. are reaped and gathered; or the outcome or consequence of any such effort or series of events. Harvest comes only after sowing. You need to understand, however, that the harvest is always more plentiful than the seed sown. You can count the number of seeds in an apple (seed time), but it is impossible to count the number of apples in a seed (harvest).

PRAYER POINTS
Prayers for Harvest of Souls

(Acts 2:14-42, 4:4)

- Worship God in the beauty of His holiness.
- Thank God for bringing many souls into the Kingdom in the past years.
- Thank God for always confirming His word, with signs and wonders, in the lives of members of the Body of Christ.

Now declare:

1. God, arise and let there be more harvest of souls in our churches this year, in the name of Jesus.

2. Father, destroy every evil arrow against genuine repentance among our members, in the name of Jesus (2 Timothy 2:26).

3. Father! Give us outstanding miracles that will draw multitudes into our churches this year, in the name of Jesus (Acts 5:11-16).

4. Father, empower your word in the mouth of all ministers to bring true repentance in the lives of sinners (Acts 2:37).

5. Father, let your grace unto salvation appear to many this year for the harvest of souls in our churches (Titus 2:11).

6. Father, make us Christ's models of good works that will invite outsiders into the fold (Titus 2:7).

7. Father, let every minister of the Gospel be a true light to their communities (Matthew 5:16).

Day 5

AND GOD SAID...

"He sent a man before them, even Joseph, who was sold for a servant: Whose feet they hurt with fetters: he was laid in iron: Until the time that his word came: the word of the LORD tried him. The king sent and loosed him; even the ruler of the people, and let him go free. He made him lord of his house, and ruler of all his substance: To bind his princes at his pleasure; and teach his senators wisdom." (Psalms 105:17-22)

This topic is huge and can be approached from many angles. However, I am persuaded to approach it this way: essentially in life, your battle moves in the direction of your tongue. Your tongue is the steering that determines ultimately where your battle will turn. Fundamentally, all battles of life are inspired and configured by words. They are also extinguished by words. All battles answer to the arrows of words – the Word of the living God.

Joseph's battles in life were tough and turbulent. He was a victim of ingrained fundamental battles. He was supposed to be Jacob's firstborn, but this fundamental battle negatively rearranged him as the eleventh son. If Jacob had married Racheal according to his plan, Joseph would have been the first son. It was the reality of the battle in place that caused the manipulation that brought Leah into Jacob's life so that Reuben came to take Joseph's place as firstborn.

Again, the battle went further to hinder Racheal from early childbearing. She was a victim of protracted delay in childbearing. The battle increased to make him suffer the loss of his mother in early childhood. The battle became more complicated as he became a victim of bitter hatred, destructive envy, and the rejection of his brethren. Everywhere he went or found himself in life, the spirit enforcing the battle monitored and remotely controlled discomfort and unpleasant experiences into his life.

However, Joseph resolved his life's battles with words – God's word. He understood and employed the winning strategy of words in winning spiritual warfare; hence the expression, *"until the time that HIS WORD came; the word of the LORD tried him"* (Psalms 105:19). Ultimately, Joseph recovered the birthright of the firstborn (1 Chronicles 5:1-2). Even when the situation was unpleasant, he kept declaring what God's word had said about him. Eventually the word prevailed (Acts 19:20).

God's word is in opposition to what the enemies or your battles are saying. Thus, when your thoughts and spoken words tally with what God has said, you will undoubtedly triumph over the battles of your life.

PRAYER POINTS

Thank God for today, thank Him for accepting our praises. Thank Him for His goodness and His wonderful works to the children of men (Psalms 107:8). Thank Him because the right hand of the LORD that doeth valiantly will rest upon our lives from now, in Jesus' name.

Bless God who has made you a masterpiece, a champion, a winner designed to make an impact. You are the head and not the tail (Deuteronomy 28:13).Plead the Blood of Jesus upon your life to cleanse and redeem you from all errors, mistakes and shortcomings.

Now declare:

1. Oh, you my destiny, enter into your season of no limit, no boundary, no barrier, as from today, in Jesus' name. As it is written in 1 Peter 2:24, I decree that by Jesus' stripes, I am healed.

2. I declare and decree by the power in the name of Jesus, I will never be submerged or be in obscurity again. I will emerge now, in the mighty name of Jesus.

3. Thou lifter of the head, my head is available, lift me up never to come down again, in Jesus' name.

4. O God of Jabez, it is my turn, enlarge my territory in Jesus' name.

5. This year, I declare that my set time of favor has come, in the mighty name of Jesus.

6. Father, my destiny is available! Make me a fisher of men, a winner of souls, a helper of the helpless, and a deliverer of captives, in Jesus' mighty name.

7. By the grace of God, I will never be small or little in life, in Jesus' name.

8. Father, waste every waster assigned against my destiny and send the captors of my star to perpetual captivity, in Jesus' name.

9. Thank you, Father, for liberating and lifting me! Blessed be your name forever and ever! Amen!

10. (Pray in tongues for several minutes and give God a loud praise. Sow your seed of deliverance).

Day 6

Yadah (Praise) God

"Oh, that men would praise (yadah) the LORD for His goodness, and for His wonderful works to the children of men" (Psalm 107:15).

Yadah is a Hebrew word for praise. Yadah is a verb with a root word which means "to throw out the hand" or "to worship with extended hand". So, to yadah is to raise our hands in praise and worship when we're in church, in the car, in our homes, or wherever we may be worshiping God.

There is something that baffles me: Why is it that when we're watching our favorite football or basketball team or a boxing match on television, we have no problem lifting our hands when our team scores a touchdown, hits a 3-pointer or kicks a field goal, but when we're in church some of us can barely get our hands out of our pockets?

Lifting our hands to God signifies two things. One, that we love God, and that we're unashamed to worship Him. Two, it is a sign of our surrender to Him as LORD of our lives. The elders have a saying, "The child with open arms gets carried by the father." When you do your part,

God will do His. 2 Chronicles 20:21 says, *"And when he had consulted with the people, he appointed those who should sing to the LORD, and who should praise the beauty of holiness, as they went out before the army and were saying: "Praise the LORD, For His mercy endures forever."*

When you praise God wholeheartedly, diverse miracles and breakthrough are abound to happen in your life, family, home, business, neighborhood and community, according to 2 Chronicles 20:17-25. The multiple possibilities of the supernatural consequences of praising God with genuine gratitude and surrender are elicited from this portion of Scripture.

PRAYER POINTS

Declare thus:

1. Father, I have reasons to praise you (go ahead and sing your reasons). Thank you for saving, healing, delivering, anointing, favoring and open doors for me. *"Break forth into joy, sing together, ye waste places of Jerusalem: for the LORD hath comforted His people, He hath redeemed Jerusalem"* (Isaiah 52:9).

2. LORD, your word says in Psalm 67:3-4, *"Let the people praise Thee, O God; let all the people praise Thee. O let the nations be glad and sing for joy…"* I declare that as I praise you, let my community and nation be glad and sing for joy.

3. LORD, your word further says in Psalm 67:5, *"Let the people praise Thee, O God; let all the people praise Thee. Then shall the earth yield her increase; and God, even our own God, shall bless us."* Father, let the earth around me yield her increase and make me swim in your blessings, in Jesus' name.

4. I command every sorrow of my heart to give way to songs of praise unto my God now, in Jesus' name.

5. Father, send me helpers of praise and worship in spirit and in truth, in Jesus' name.

6. I relocate from the camp of grumblers to the yadah camp, in Jesus' name.

7. Every agenda of sorrow and tragedy drawn up by my enemy is destroyed and shall neither stand nor come to pass, in Jesus' name.

8. I declare loud and clear that the joy of the LORD is my strength! (Nehemiah 8:10).

9. As the LORD lives and my soul lives, no one in my family will shed tears of sorrow this year and in the years to come, in Jesus' name. Joy, laughter, celebrations, songs of praise and adoration shall perpetually be heard in my family.

10. O LORD, I have sown in tears long enough; let me begin to reap the harvest of worship, praise and adoration from now on, in Jesus' name (Psalm 126:1-6).

11. *"Let everything that has breath praise the LORD – Praise the LORD!"* (Psalm 150:6)

12. (Praise Him for answered worship, adoration, thanksgiving and praise!)

Day 7

MORE THAN

CONQUERORS

"Nay, in all these things we are more than conquerors through Him that loved us." (Romans 8:37)

It is a great thing to be a conqueror in the Christian life and in conflict. It is a much greater thing to be more than a conqueror "in all these things" which the apostle names - a combination of trials, troubles and foes. But what does it mean to be "more than a conqueror"?

It means to have a decisive victory. There are some victories that cost nearly as much as defeat and more of such seeming triumphs could destroy the victor. There are some battles that get renewed until the fighters are exhausted by the ceaseless strife. However, it is possible to settle the questions that meet us, one by one, and settle them forever.

It is to have such a victory as will effectually break the adversary's power. That is, not only defend us from his attacks but effectually weaken and destroy his strength. This is one of the purposes of temptation, that we may be workers together with God in destroying evil. Look at Moses and the Egyptians. It was not enough for Israel to beat them off and be saved from their attacks; God wanted them exterminated. Therefore, God allows tempters to be provoked into activity in order to challenge our resistance and lead to our aggressive and victorious advance against them.

It is to have such a victory that brings actual benefit out of the battle and makes it tributary to our own and our Master's cause. That act of God brought Moses into Pharaoh's house and raised up a deliverer for Israel, and the destroyer of Pharaoh. Surely Satan was more than beaten at Calvary! His most audacious attempt was the crucifixion of our LORD, and all hell, no doubt, held high jubilee on that dark afternoon when Jesus sank to death; but lo! the cross has become the weapon by which Satan's head is already bruised and his kingdom is being exterminated. So, God makes him forge the weapons of his own destruction and hurl the thunderbolts that fall back upon his own head.

It is not only to have the victory, but to possess the spoils of victory. When Jehoshaphat's army won their great deliverance from the hordes of Moab and Ammon, it took them three days to gather all the spoils of their enemies' camps. When David captured the camp of Ziklag's destroyers, he won so vast a booty that he was able to send rich presents over all Israel among his brethren. When the lepers found their way to the deserted camp of the Syrians, they found such abundance that in a single hour the famine of Samaria was turned into satiety. And so, our spiritual conflicts and conquests have their rich reward in the treasures recovered from the hands of the enemy.

It means not only to win your battle and save your territory, but to do honor to your Captain and your God; to be a credit to your cause and affirm yourself in the campaign that God shall be glorified. Many of our battles are fought in view of heaven alone. That is the strange picture that Paul the apostle gives of his trials, "We are made a gazing-stock to angels and principalities" (Hebrews 10:33).

It means having both earthly and eternal victory; that is, victory that includes final triumph and eternal reward. How Heaven will recompense her victors some glorious day! So now, die to a self-seeking disposition; die to the preferring of public opinion over the voice of the Living God, and die to selfish ambition and vain conceit. God doesn't use men that are alive. He uses men that are dead. He doesn't use sober men. He uses drunk men. He doesn't use somebody. He uses nobody.

"In all these things..." What's your point of defeat right now? Is it prayerlessness, a lack of love, self-pity, self-seeking, self-glory, or self-promoting? What is it? You'll have to confess it, as I can't do that for you.

PRAYER POINTS

- Thank God for today, tomorrow and eternity. Thank Him for Jesus; thank Him for the Holy Spirit; thank

Him for His Word. Thank Him for changing your story by the death of His Son at Calvary! Hallelujah!

- Plead the Blood of Jesus upon your body, soul and spirit for redemption and forgiveness from all sins and deliverance from the sins that easily beset you.

Now, make these declarations:

1. This day, I command, and I receive power to pursue, overtake and recover all losses of the past years in my life, family and church, in Jesus' name.

2. Every power that is breaking or annulling the scriptures, as well as resisting prophecies in my life, be devoured by fire now.

3. I curse every stranger, parasite, tare, disobedience and devourer that is operating in any area of my life and destiny, in Jesus' name. Anointing to be ten-times better, fall on me as from today, in Jesus' name

4. Anointing for distinction, excellence and dominion, fall on me now by fire, in Jesus' name.

5. The anointing to be above and not beneath, power for uncommon lifting, the reigning and ruling anointing, fall on me as from today, in Jesus' name.

6. Every force and power that is challenging and contesting my power of being "more than a conqueror," be consumed by fire, in Jesus' name.

7. The "more than conquerors" anointing, baptize me, fall on me and consume from my life the yoke of bondage and being dominated as from today, in Jesus' name.

8. Remember to pray for our spiritual father and mother, Daddy and Mummy G.O. for the grace to continually win, to stay strong in body, soul and spirit. Pray that they will not be weary or tired, in Jesus' name, and that the anointing over their lives shall be perpetually fresh, in Jesus' name.

Thank God for answered prayers.

Day 8

SHOUTS OF JOY

"And when the ark of the covenant of the LORD came into the camp, all Israel shouted with a great shout, so that the earth rang again. And when the Philistines heard the noise of the shout, they said, What meaneth the noise of this great shout in the camp of the Hebrews? And they understood that the ark of the LORD was come into the camp. And the Philistines were afraid, for they said, God is come into the camp. And they said, Woe unto us! for there hath not been such a thing heretofore. Woe unto us! who shall deliver us out of the hand of these mighty Gods? these are the Gods that smote the Egyptians with all the plagues in the wilderness." (1 Samuel 4:5-8)

There is power in the shout of the children of God.

- It was a shout that brought down the walls of Jericho (Joshua 6:20).

- It was a shout that put an end to the siege over Samaria (2 Kings 7:6).

- The shout of Paul and Silas, in praises and prayers, in the prison was so loud that the sleeping prisoners heard them. Moreover, it was so loud that it caused an earthquake that forced the prison doors opened (Acts 16:25-26).

As you shout for joy this day, every wall of Jericho shall fall flat, an end shall come to every siege and the prison doors shall be forced opened, in Jesus' name.

Rejoicing gives access to:

- *"...draw[ing] water out of the wells of salvation"* (Isaiah 12:3).
- The better things happening after salvation (Hebrews 12:24).
- God's presence (Psalms 124; 16:11).
- God's strength (Nehemiah 8:10).
- God's voice – God speaks and ministers to you (Isaiah 30:29-30).
- Victory over your enemy (1 Chronicles 20:21-24).
- Deliverance (Acts 16:25-26).
- Divine health. Proverbs 17:22 says, *"A merry heart doeth good like medicine..."*

PRAYER POINTS

- Praise the LORD with a loud shout and welcome His presence where you are now.

Now pray thus:

1. Father, in the name of Jesus, I repent of every sin in my life, please don't let my joy be replaced with sorrow.

2. Father, let there be fear and trembling in the camp of my enemies throughout this year, in Jesus' name.

3. Father, let there be a shaking tonight that shakes off any evil thing deposited in my body, in the name of Jesus.

4. O God, arise in your power and confuse all my oppressors, in Jesus' name.

5. Father, let me experience the fullness of your joy throughout this year, in Jesus' name.

6. Father, let the adversaries receive a sign that you are present in my life and my family throughout this year that they may steer clear of us, in Jesus' name.

7. Father, make me a wonder throughout this year, in Jesus' name.

Day 9

DREAMLIKE
MIRACLES

When the LORD brought back the captivity of Zion, We were like those who dream Then our mouth was filled with laughter, And our tongue with singing. Then they said among the nations, "The LORD has done great things for them." The LORD has done great things for us, And we are glad. (Psalm 126:1-4)

Some contemporary scholars have described dreams as mere myths; figments of people's imaginations and sometimes illusions. To them, dreams are fantasies, pictorial metaphors which were semi-consciously put together by human senses. However, the truth is that in these last days, God is revealing more of Himself through the ministry of the Holy Spirit. God speaks through His word; as well as through prophecy, preaching, through your wife, husband, children and yes, through dreams. Numbers 12:6, says "...*if there be a prophet among you, I the LORD will make myself known unto him in a vision, and will speak to him in a dream.*"

BUT NOT ALL DREAMS COME FROM GOD! Psalms 126:1-5 is both a testimonial and a prophecy. It is about the deliverance of God's people from Babylon back to Zion. This day, you will leave Babylon and enter Zion in Jesus' name! "*WHEN the LORD turned the captivity of*

Zion..." (v.1a) This shows that there is a divine timing for your turnaround. There is a time appointed for your release. It is now! Total emancipation from captivity is not subject to probability. It is certain. It is a matter of time and the time is now.

We can't really explain why the people of Zion went into captivity. It may be because of their sin. However, one thing is clear; their movement into captivity was not for their destruction but to teach them a lesson. It was not for the purpose of consuming them as dross is consumed in a fire but for their transformation, just as gold passes through fire so that it can shine better. God's plan for you is that you be like Christ (2 Corinthians 3:18). No matter how much you look up to man, if the LORD does not help you, no one else can. It was after the LORD stepped into the situation of Zion that there was a turnaround.

PRAYER POINTS

- Thank God for today. Thank Him because the days, weeks, months and years ahead of you are blessed. He is mighty and strong to save, redeem and deliver you.

- Plead the Blood of Jesus - for mercy, atonement and redemption.

Now, declare:

1. Every curse that makes a man to have evil dreams come to pass and good dreams fail, break now upon my life by fire in Jesus' name.

2. Every power that is manipulating my dream life, be devoured now by fire in Jesus' name.

3. Every pollution, confusion, congestion and perversion of my mind, clear now by fire in Jesus' name.

4. Anointing of the super achievers, fall on me now by fire in Jesus' name.

5. Oh God, set the ladder of greatness and distinction for me as from today in Jesus' name.

6. Every power that is making the status quo my normal order of life, be devoured now by fire in Jesus' name.

7. Every yoke of domination, oppression and affliction upon my life and destiny, break now by fire in Jesus' name.

8. Power to be a voice, not an echo; a solution, not a problem; an answer, not a question; an asset, not a liability, fall on me now in Jesus' name.

9. Every dream killer that is monitoring my life and destiny, die now by fire in Jesus' name.

10. I decree that as from today, I refuse the evil and choose the good throughout my journey on earth in Jesus' name.

Day 10

EXTREME
MAKEOVER

"Remember ye not the former things, neither consider the things of old. Behold, I will do a new thing; now it shall spring forth; shall ye not know it? I will even make a way in the wilderness, and rivers in the desert." (Isaiah 43:18-19)

God remains in the business of extreme makeovers. That is, transforming the lives of people who have surrendered themselves to Him. The LORD picks up a person, regardless of how bad they have been, works in them, fills them with His Spirit and transforms them to the most wonderful person they can ever be. This process itself brings glory to God.

Genuine transformation is what brings glory to God when people see it (Matthew 5:16). Transformation doesn't occur automatically. As God is doing His work, we must also act correspondingly. Our work begins where God's ends. Our efforts are secondary to the primary work done by God. However, it is a necessary accompaniment, and when this is done, the result is a transformed life that brings glory and honor to our Father in heaven. That is the real "extreme makeover."

The finished product of transformation is Christlikeness. God wants to produce Christ in every one of us. May

God give us the understanding and appropriation of His grace in our lives to become His intended product – little Christs.

PRAYER POINTS

Pray thus:

1. Father, I thank you because you are my Shepherd and I shall not want or lack any good thing in my life.

2. I repent of having tried to work things out myself by the arm of flesh. I ask for your forgiveness and mercy, in Jesus' name.

3. Good health, profitable businesses, a Holy Spirit-filled life and church, and a fruitful marriage are all good things. Your Word says you will not withhold any good thing from those who walk uprightly (Psalm 84:11). I claim this promise for my life, in Jesus' name.

4. I petition that Christ's resurrection power fall upon my marital, physical, spiritual, ecclesiastical, and financial destinies now, in Jesus' name.

5. Dear LORD, open my eyes to see any irritating or offensive behavior, bad attitude, nauseating character traits or disposition in me, and grant me the grace to deal effectively with them, in Jesus' name.

6. Every power that has vowed to die instead of seeing my glory ahead, you are snared by your words. May your death be swift, in Jesus' name.

7. I decree, like the Shunammite woman (2 Kings 4:26), that it is well with my wife, my husband, my children, my family, my church, my city and my nation, in Jesus' name.

8. Like Solomon, I shall enjoy rest; my life shall not be characterized by endless battles, in Jesus' name.

9. Right now, I command my glory to be awakened, and to shine for all to see, in Jesus' name.

10. I thank you, Father, for giving me victory over every unfinished battle of my family line, in Jesus' name.

11. Every destiny project I embark upon this year shall witness successful completion, in the mighty name of Jesus.

12. Thank you, Father, that by your grace, I shall be singing songs of victory throughout this year and beyond, in Jesus' name.

Day 11

GLORY AHEAD

To whom God would make known what is the riches of the glory of this mystery among the Gentiles; which is Christ in you, the hope of glory. (Colossians 1:27)

As stated in the above verse, if Christ is in you, glory is ahead for you! This portion of Scripture is a missile for the termination of losses, disappointments, delays, denials, shame and misfortunes of the past years in your life. Glories that have been diseased, tampered with, captured, and manipulated shall be freed, delivered, and celebrated this year, in Jesus' name. By His word, you will get back all that Satan has stolen from your life, family, business, church, and ministry, in Jesus' name. In this new year, understand that 'Glory Ahead' is a manifesto. That manifesto has practical meaning for our daily lives, such as that it:

- Prophesies divine repositioning. (Psalms 3:3).

- It's a word of encouragement for strength in one's spirit. (2 Corinthians 4:17).

- Promises protection from seen and unseen personalities or situations. (Isaiah 4:5).

- Connotes victory in Jesus. It says that tomorrow will be better than today, with the promise of testimonies around the corner. (Psalms 30:5).

- Implies that while things seem good now, they can get even better as the LORD lifts them to higher levels of glory. (2 Corinthians 3:18).

- Means that, at long last, you will sing a new song. (Isaiah 42:9-10).

- Assures of no more shame, failures will be forgotten, and there will be no more dejected bowing of the head. (Joel 2:26)

Israel's journey through the wilderness from Egypt to the land flowing with milk and honey was glory - powered and orchestrated for 40 years (Exodus 40:34-38). They were not allowed to be defeated or molested; they had been marked by 'glory ahead.' "Touch not mine anointed and do my prophets no harm." (Psalms 105:15)

There is a glory that awaits you this year, but you must arise and wage war by praying the following prayers repeatedly and aggressively. They are for your glory to arise and shine. It is written in Zechariah 9:11-12 that, *"As for thee also, by the blood of thy covenant I have sent forth thy prisoners out of the pit wherein is no water. Turn you to the strong hold, ye prisoners of hope: even today do I declare that I will render double unto thee."* Also, Proverbs 6:5 says, "Deliver thyself as a roe from the hand of the hunter, and as a bird from the hand of the fowler."

PRAYER POINTS

Pray thus:

1. Father, thank you for your faithfulness. You are my Maker, Lover, my King and my Creator. Thank you because your word is forever settled and will never return void. Thank you!

2. I hereby confess every sin, personal, generational or ancestral that has made anyone in my family tree, including myself, candidates of obscurity.

3. I hereby receive a fresh baptism of the Holy Spirit into my spirit man, in the mighty name of Jesus.

4. Wake up, my glory! Begin to attract unlimited grace, favor, helpers, wealth transfer, honor, abundance, fresh anointing, peace, respect, breakthrough, success, testimonies, and new open doors of opportunities, in Jesus' name.

5. I command my glory to reject the activities of glory hunters and sin, in Jesus' name.

6. Every Satanic conspiracy against my glory, be nullified by the Blood of Jesus.

7. Father, I pray that my glory begins to attract goodness, in Jesus' name. It shall not be captured by the devil, in Jesus' name.

8. My glory shall not be manipulated and bewitched, in Jesus' name, because it rejects sin and every agent of the devil. My glory shall not be sick or diseased, in Jesus' name.

9. My crown of glory will not be stolen, in Jesus' name. I command my glory to return to me, in Jesus' name.

10. My glory is recovered and shall begin to shine from henceforth, in Jesus' name. Fire of God, envelope my glory, in Jesus' name.

11. This year, I shall arise from story to glory, from labor to favor, from shame to fame, from Marah to Naomi, from sorrow to joy, from pressure to pleasure, from trials to triumph, from tribulation to testimonies, and from problem to promotion, in Jesus' name!

12. As a glory carrier, I decree from henceforth, that my full rights and entitlements be delivered to me, in Jesus' name.

13. Father, thank you for answers to my prayers; for the restoration and manifestation of my glory, in Jesus' name. Amen.

Day 12

BLESSED FAMILY

"For this cause shall a man leave his father and mother, and shall be joined unto his wife, and they two shall be one flesh.." (Ephesians 5:31)

Marriage is the lifelong union of a man and a woman under God, both of whom are living, growing, and changing for God's glory (Genesis 2:22-24; Proverbs 20:6-7). If any of these ingredients are missing, abuse of original intent is inevitable. *"Haven't you read," he replied, "that at the beginning the Creator 'made them male and female,' and said, 'For this reason a man will leave his father and mother and be united to his wife, and the two will become one flesh'? So, they are no longer two, but one flesh. Therefore, what God has joined together, let no one separate."* (Matthew 19:4-6, NIV)

People get married for different reasons, which include social, financial and cultural demands, as well as peer pressure, family expectations etc. However, there is a biblical reason for God's institution of marriage. Faithfulness and blamelessness reflected in the character of the LORD Jesus Christ are key (Ephesians 5:22-33).

Marriage is a journey by ship i.e. a voyage. Regular ships have two licensed captains with one being The Captain while the other is the Staff Captain, or second-in-command. This is like a plane having a pilot and a copilot. The ship of the marriage voyage requires the deep involvement of three parties i.e. the husband, the wife, and God. All parties must work by a defined protocol to ensure the ship arrives at its destination intended by God, the author of marriage (Romans 12:1-2; Ephesians 5:24-27). A lack of understanding of, and adherence to, God's foundational principles result in the alarming rate of dysfunctional and failed marriage relationships we see in our world today.

PRAYER POINTS

Declare thus:

1. Dear Heavenly Father, I thank you for your mercy that has preserved my life. Thank you for keeping me alive today and in good health. I thank you for your gift of life to me and my loved ones. Blessed be your holy name, in Jesus' name.

2. On the authority of your word in 3 John 2, from now on, I start to experience all-round progress in my life, destiny, health, marriage, career, business, and ministry, in Jesus' name.

3. Dear Heavenly Father, according to your word in Isaiah 57:14, I come against every form of demonic stumbling blocks and satanic strongholds that have constituted obstacles to my advancement and that of my family; they are hereby totally demolished, in Jesus' name.

4. I speak against every evil garment and satanic apparel that the enemy has put upon me or my loved ones in the realm of the spirit that may have limited or hindered our progress. I command such to catch fire and be burnt to ashes now, in Jesus' name.

5. Isaiah 8:18 says, *"Here am I and the children whom the LORD has given me! We are for signs and wonders in Israel from the LORD of Hosts, who dwells in Mount Zion"* (NIV). Therefore, I and mine shall receive the goodness of the LORD. 1 Chronicles 13:14 says, *"And the ark of God remained with the family of Obed-edom in his house three months. And the LORD blessed the house of Obed-edom, and all that he had."* LORD, as you blessed the family of Obed-edom, bless my family too, in Jesus' name.

6. Father, whatever hindered and delayed me in the past shall not hinder my progress and advancement in 2020 and beyond, in Jesus' name. The curse of hindrance over my life, family, and children is completely uprooted now, in the name of Jesus.

7. Father, you supernaturally accelerated the advancement of Prophet Elijah in 1 Kings 18:46 and he was able to outrun a chariot; divinely accelerate progress for me and my loved ones from now on, in Jesus' name.

(Remember to pray for your Pauls, Timothys and Barnabases - mentors, mentees, colleagues).

Thank God for prayers answered.

Day 13

THE VOICE OF GOD

"Day unto day uttereth speech, and night unto night sheweth knowledge. There is no speech nor language, where their voice is not heard." "The law of the LORD is perfect, converting the soul: the testimony of the LORD is sure, making wise the simple. The statutes of the LORD are right, rejoicing the heart: the commandment of the LORD is pure, enlightening the eyes." (Psalm 19:2-3, 7-8)

There are several words used to describe the word of God: The law; the testimony; the statues and the commandments.

In the above verses there are two revelations of God expressed:

General Revelation: One of the ways God speaks to us is in verses 2 and 3. He speaks to us through general revelation. The general revelation is what God gives to us through creation. That is, without anybody talking to us about God, creation itself speaks to us. If you leave humans in any environment, in any cultures, in any planet, leave them alone, without anybody talking to them about God, without any education, without any bible, without any religion, leave humans in their natural state – they will end up with a concept that there is a God. The knowledge of God is natural to man. The reason for this is that creation speaks to us about God. When there is a creation, you draw up a conclusion that there is a creator.

Special Revelation: This is the second way God speaks to us. This is God revealed in Word; What God has spoken. God speaks through creation (General Revelation); He speaks through His written word (Special Revelation). This is what we call the Bible. It is the law of the LORD. It is the testimony of the LORD, it is the statutes of the LORD. It is the commandment of God. When we read special revelation, it must lead us to God.

The agent God uses to open our eyes to Himself through general revelation and special revelation is the Holy Spirit.

The Holy Spirit helps us to know God. (2 Corinthians 13:14). The trinity is present in this verse. "The grace of the LORD Jesus Christ", this is God the Son. "The love of God," God the father; "the communion of the Holy Spirit", God the Holy Spirit. If you look at the personalities of the trinity, something is assigned to them. To God the father, is love. God the father, reveals love. *For God so loved that He gave His only begotten son.* If you want to experience grace, it is through Jesus Christ. The law came through Moses, grace and truth came through Jesus Christ (Jn. 1:17; 1:14). What is assigned to the Holy Spirit is fellowship. If you want fellowship with God, you must know the Holy Spirit. To experience grace is through the Son, to experience love, it is through the Father and to experience genuine fellowship, it is through the Holy Spirit.

PRAYER POINTS

Offer thanksgiving prayers to God for keeping you standing today, regardless of what you have been through (Psalm 105:24, Lamentations 3.21-22). Thank God for giving you a new year, a new month, and a new day. Thank God for giving you a new beginning.

Now declare:

1. Father, on the authority of your word in Jeremiah 7:23, I repent of every form of spiritual carelessness, disobedience, stubbornness, that could have kept me backward in the journey of life; have mercy on me, in Jesus' name.

2. Father, on the authority of your word in Job 8:20, I repent of all my careless choices that could have made you withdraw your help, grace and favor for my advancement in the journey of life, in Jesus' name.

3. Father, from now on, as I hear and obey your word, I shall make progress in leaps and bounds in this year and beyond. I shall move forward, onward, and upward, in Jesus' name.

4. Father, on the authority of your word in 3 John 2, from now on, I start to experience all round progress

in my life, destiny, health, marriage, career, business, and ministry, in Jesus' name.

5. Father, on the authority of your word in 1Samuel 30:8, as I discern your word, release upon me the anointing to pursue, catch up, overtake and recover all my lost grounds, opportunities and possessions in life, in Jesus' name.

6. Father, according to your word in Isaiah 48:17, teach me to make profit from my efforts in life, and supernaturally direct me in the way to go, in Jesus' name.

7. Father, I thank you for answering my prayers; blessed be your holy name, O God! Amen.

Day 14

VESSELS OF HONOR

"But in a great house there are not only vessels of gold and silver, but also of wood and clay, some for honor and some for dishonor. Therefore if anyone cleanses himself from the latter, he will be a vessel for honor, sanctified and useful for the Master, prepared for every good work." (2 Timothy 2:20-21)

Vessels of honor and dishonor, as well as their characteristics, are described in 2 Timothy 2:19-25. How a vessel is used and to what use it is put determines if it is a container of esteemed or contempt. Timothy was making daily decisions that determined what type of vessel he would prove to be in God's house. So are we! *"Those who cleanse themselves… will be instruments for special purposes, made holy, useful to the Master and prepared to do any good work"* (2 Timothy 2:21, NIV). The type of vessel you choose to be in the house of God has eternal consequences!

According to 2 Corinthians 6:16, the church is a great house belonging to a great God purchased at Calvary, according to the promise, *"I will dwell in them and walk in them"* (2 Corinthians 6:16c). The church is the temple in which the LORD is worshipped, the palace in which He rules, the mansion in which He abides (Psalm 132:14). It is His castle, the place of defense for His truth, and the armory from which He supplies His people with weapons. Therefore, we must respect God and ourselves by how we behave in the house of God (1 Timothy 3:15, NLT). Each one of us must choose what type of vessel we want to be in God's house – whether of honor or dishonor.

PRAYER POINTS

On the inspiration of Psalms 124, if God had not been on our side so far we could have been thirsty, with no water to drink. We could have entered into trouble and found no one to help. We could have lifted our hands and found them withered or even join the congregation of the dead. Because of His everlasting love and unchanging faithfulness, bless Him, thank Him, bless His Holy Name. Thank Him for making us part of a covenant to prepare a people for Himself that propagate the gospel of Christ to the uttermost parts of the earth.

Now, pray thus:

1. Holy Ghost fire, purge my heart of every unforgiveness, in Jesus' name. Eradicate every form of bitterness from my heart, in Jesus' name.

2. Father, make me a vessel unto honor, break me, mold me and use me for your glory, in Jesus' name.

3. I reject every spirit of error, mistakes, and cyclically falling into sin and rising, in Jesus' name.

4. I bind the spirit of depression, frustration and disillusionment in my life, in Jesus' name.

5. LORD, prepare me as a sanctuary: pure and holy, tried and true for you, in Jesus' name.

6. I bind the spirit of servitude to sin, Satan, worldly standards and persuasions in my life, in Jesus' name.

7. Let every taskmaster supervising and subjecting me to hard labor be roasted by the fire of the Holy Ghost, in the Name of Jesus.

8. Father don't let me lose my focus on you in all my undertakings, in Jesus' name.

9. Almighty Father make your church a new threshing instrument with sharp teeth to tear apart every enemy on her way, in Jesus' name. (Isaiah 41:15)Thank you, LORD, for answered prayers, in Jesus' name.

Day 15

DOMINION MANDATE

"And God blessed them, and God said unto them, be fruitful, and multiply, and replenish the earth, and subdue it: and have dominion over the fish of the sea, and over the fowl of the air, and over every living thing that moves upon the earth." (Genesis 1:22)

O ur focus for this day is the privileges of the dominion mandate available to the divine champion. We need to understand what accrues to us. What are the possessions that become reality in our lives due to our relationship with Jesus Christ? The dominion mandate, of which we speak, is clearly outlined in Genesis 1:22. It says, *"And God blessed them, and God said unto them, be fruitful, and multiply, and replenish the earth, and subdue it: and have dominion over the fish of the sea, and over the fowl of the air, and over every living thing that moves upon the earth."* These riches, rights, and privileges are a constant theme throughout the Bible.

The book of Ephesians talks repeatedly about the "surpassing riches" of Christ's grace that has already been lavished on us, enriching our lives (Ephesians 1:7-8, 2:7, 3:8). In fact, Philippians 4:19 says, "My God shall supply all your needs according to His riches in glory through Christ Jesus." There is much in the New Testament about the riches that is ours; accrued to us by The Anointed One and His anointing.

However, these privileges are accompanied by responsibilities that are clearly stated in both the Old and New Testaments of the Holy Bible. In Deuteronomy 7:6, we read that we are a people holy unto the LORD, chosen by Him that He may lavish His love on us because we were nothing when He found us. This makes it imperative that we listen to, and obey, God's instructions, ensuring the continuity of enjoying these privileges instead of being returned to zero. In consonance, 1 Peter 2:9 asserts that we are a "chosen generation (God's special possession, NLT), a royal priesthood, a holy nation, a peculiar (or obviously unique) people. Why? All these responsibilities are ours solely to "show forth the praises of Him who has called us out of darkness into His marvelous light."

It would be a wicked insult to God for you to stand before Him at the end of this life unnoticed, unknown, unsung, unannounced and uncelebrated by Heaven.

PRAYER POINTS

Offer thanksgiving to God for all that God has done and He is doing.

Now, declare:

1. I plead the Blood of Jesus for forgiveness and mercy to purify and sanctify. I receive power to sin no more.

This month and forever, your kingdom come; your will be done in my life, in Jesus' name.

2. Because of the dominion mandate, I receive power for expansion and enlargement, breakthrough and break forth in all areas of my life as from today, in Jesus' name.

3. I receive Amos 9:13 into my life. I decree that these are the days of my life that the plowman shall overtake the reaper, and the treader of grapes him that soweth seed; and the mountains shall drop sweet wine, and all the hills shall melt, in Jesus' name.

4. Joseph had to come out from prison for him to unite with his brothers in his glory. I rebuke every fowl spirit of imprisonment over my life. I come out from every form of imprisonment now, in Jesus' name.

5. Thou garment of forgetfulness, reproach, disgrace and shame upon my life and destiny, tear by fire, in Jesus' name.

6. I receive right now the magnetic anointing that attracts help, divine connection, divine collection, favour and all the pleasant things of life, in Jesus' name.

7. According to 1 Kings 18:46, Father, let your hand be upon me for exploits, in Jesus' name.

8. Power for a bumper harvest in all my ventures in life, fall upon me now by fire, in Jesus' name.

9. I prophesy that where the good from my life has been forgotten before, I shall be remembered & rewarded for good as from today, in Jesus' name.

Day 16

FROM GLORY TO GLORY

"But we all, with unveiled face, beholding as in a mirror the glory of the LORD, are being transformed into the same image from glory to glory, just as from the LORD, the Spirit." (2 Corinthians 3:18)

"For thus saith the LORD of hosts; Yet once, it is a little while, and I will shake the heavens, and the earth...I will fill this house with glory, saith the LORD of hosts. The silver is mine, and the gold is mine, saith the LORD of hosts." (Haggai 2:6-8)

With these few words, "from glory to glory," Paul sums up our entire Christian life – from redemption, to sanctification, to baptism in the Holy Spirit (with the evidence of speaking in tongues), to daily being transformed into the image of God's own beloved Son on earth, and finally to our glorious eternal welcome into heaven. This is the invitation the LORD makes to all Christians, to have our lives radically transformed here and now, by opening our eyes to see the glorious journey He is taking us on "from glory to glory."

The angels in heaven wondered about the love God has for humanity, and the question finally came out in Psalms 8:4-5, *"What is man that thou art mindful of him, and the son of man, that thou visitest him? For thou has made him a little lower than the angels and crowned him with glory and honor.*" According to the constitution and plan of heaven for your life, you are supposed to be covered and walking in glory and honor; shame and dishonor are not part of God's plan for your life. You are meant to be a victor and not a victim, and live a life that brings honor and glory to God daily. I pray that the Almighty put on you again the crown of glory you have lost to the enemy, in Jesus' name!

What is Glory? Glory is the opposite of shame. It is the shining beauty of God upon a woman. Glory reveals the supernatural nature and the ability of God in the life of a man. 1 John 4:17 says, "*Herein is our love made perfect, that we may have boldness in the day of judgment: because as He is, so are we in this world.*" Your background notwithstanding, you can live a glorious and honorable full life. It is your right; say it! Do not resign yourself to fate; exercise your faith! Do not let go of your divine inheritance. God gave glory back to you at Calvary, do not hand it over to the devil again.

PRAYER POINTS

Declare thus:

1. Father, I thank you that you had me in mind at creation. I am neither an afterthought nor an accident. Thank you, LORD!

2. LORD, restore my former glory. Everything that is mine, I take back, in Jesus' name. Let me glorify you as I daily walk with you, in Jesus' name.

3. Father, strip me of every filthy garment put on me by the devil and set it ablaze, in Jesus' name. LORD, I thank you that you are my advocate in every matter of accusation the devil brings up against me before the Father (Romans 8:34).

4. Father, put on me again the crown of glory and honor, in Jesus' name. No more shame, embarrassment, dishonor, or stigma, in Jesus' name. As from today, I will occupy the seat of honor and glory meant for me, in Jesus' name.

5. I reject the spirit of, and the desire for, sin and all willful disobedience to God's Word that results in poverty, lack, and insufficiency, in Jesus' name.

6. I break the yoke of perpetually falling into sin, as well as the yoke of begging and continually getting loans, off my life, in Jesus' name. I will lend to nations, I am the head and not the tail, and the glory of the LORD shall shine forth in my life, in Jesus' name (Isaiah 60:1-3).

7. Every wealth of mine locked up in the enemy's stronghold is set free today by the fire of the Holy Ghost, in Jesus' name.

8. Father, please help me to please you all the days of my life. Keep me pure and holy!

9. Exodus 22:7 says, "If a man shall deliver unto his neighbor money or stuff to keep, and it be stolen out of the man's house; if the thief be found, let him pay double." The thief is the devil (John 10:10), and I demand double for all the enemy has stolen, in Jesus' name.

Thank God for answered prayers.

Day 17

DIVINE VICTORY

"Then the men of the city said to Elisha, "Please notice, the situation of this city is pleasant, as my lord sees; but the water is bad, and the ground barren." And he said, "Bring me a new bowl, and put salt in it." So, they brought it to him. Then he went out to the source of the water, and cast in the salt there, and said, "Thus says the LORD: 'I have healed this water; from it there shall be no more death or barrenness." (2 Kings 2:19-21)

In the book of Zechariah, Zerubbabel, the governor of Judah, and all Judah were so frightened because the adversaries had vowed that the temple would never be built. Instead, the LORD sent the prophet Zechariah to Zerubbabel with the promise of divine assistance and success. Zechariah 4:6 says, *"Not by might nor by power, but by My Spirit,' says the LORD Almighty."* Are you on a building project and surrounded by adversaries? Are you so discouraged that you want to give up? Are the enemies, the Sanballats and Tobiahs, of this world saying, "You shall not do it?" Forget their threats, railings, taunts or accusations. In Zerubbabel's case, it was consequent upon the threat of the enemies that God sent the message of deliverance, guaranteeing victory, through the prophet.

There are a lot of people in life whose lives appear pleasant (like Jericho), yet their daily experiences are bitter and barren. They are beautiful, handsome, skilled, educated, ingenious, resourceful and hardworking, yet no commensurate results to match their efforts. They live insignificant and a meaningless lives. For example, he's anointed but cannot seem to succeed in ministry. This is another Jericho. However, by His Spirit, victory is guaranteed this day, in Jesus' name, I pray for you that the error and fault in your foundations will be healed, and the source of water for your destiny will be sweetened again, by His Spirit, in Jesus' name!

PRAYER POINTS

Begin to thank God for your life, for another year and for the divine victory Jesus purchased for us by His blood at Calvary. Thank Him for your yesterdays, today, and tomorrows.

Now, declare:

1. Father, you are my Jehovah-Nissi (Exodus 17:15); please weaken the hands of anyone raising any banner up against me, in Jesus' name. Every rod of wickedness raised up against me shall be reduced to ashes, in Jesus' name.

2. Father, please, give me a new song of victory to sing this month, in Jesus' name.

3. Holy Spirit, please strengthen and empower me against recurrent or ongoing battles in my life, in Jesus' name. Dear Holy Spirit, according to Isaiah 10:27, please lift every satanic burden off me, and break and destroy every yoke off my shoulders by the anointing, in Jesus' name.

4. Whatsoever is caging my gifting, skills, and endowments, causing them not to work and produce for me, be consumed by fire, in the name of the LORD Jesus Christ (Isaiah 32:13-15).

5. Father, let me drink of the Holy Spirit's River of Life (John 7:38) that I may be watered as the garden of Eden; experiencing continuous freshness in life and ministry (1 Samuel 10:6). Make me a man after God's own heart, fulfilling Your every purpose for my life, in Jesus' name (Acts 13:22).

6. May the packages the LORD deposited in my life, even before I was conceived in my mother's womb, begin to manifest corresponding results as from today, in Jesus' name.

7. As from today, I prophesy that I will begin to live a life of growth, meaning, and glory, in Jesus' name.

Day 18

THE BALM OF GILEAD

"Is there no balm in Gilead; is there no physician there? why then is not the health of the daughter of My people recovered?" (Jeremiah 8:22)

B alm was first used as a preservative and later in indigenous remedies meant to heal and soothe. Embalming took its name from the use of balm as a preservative in earlier times. Both Jacob and Joseph were embalmed by the Egyptian method: *"And Joseph commanded his servants the physicians to embalm his father..."* (Genesis 50:2-3). *"So, Joseph died...and they embalmed him, and he was put in a coffin in Egypt."* (Genesis 50:24-26).

Biblical history states that the area of Gilead was rich in spices and aromatic gums that provided balm, which was then exported to Egypt, Tyre, and the land of Israel. But spiritually viewed, what is this balm? It is JESUS and His all-powerful blood!

When Adam [and the Church of God within him] fell upon the rocks of sin and temptation, he shipwrecked the image of God in which he had been created. And as water floods into a shipwrecked vessel, so sin rushed into every faculty of his body and soul, penetrating the inmost recesses of his being.

However, the frightful havoc sin makes is neither seen nor felt until the soul is quickened into spiritual life. It is the sword of the Spirit which cuts and wounds; it is the entrance of life and light that gashes the conscience. It is the divine work of quickening to life that lacerates the heart and inflicts those deep wounds which nothing but the "balm in Gilead" can heal.

As previously established, balm preserves. However, Jesus preserves eternally (John 3:16; Hebrews 7:25; 1Peter 2:23-24). *In Mark 2:17,* the bible introduces JESUS as the physician. "Balm in Gilead" therefore connotes "preservation, healing, soothing and recovery in Jesus."

Why the peculiar line of questioning in Jeremiah 8:22 then? "Is there no balm in Gilead? *Is there no physician there? Why then is not the health of the daughter of my people recovered?" Jeremiah 8:22.* This line of questioning is fraught with pain, worry, confusion, concern and desperation. These questions were posed by the prophet, Jeremiah, under unique circumstances that elicited very peculiar and painful feelings. Why was he hurt and wounded in spirit though?

PRAYER POINTS

Declare:

1. I bless your name, O LORD. I confess that you are the LORD, the Balm in Gilead, the Rose of Sharon, the Lily of the Valley. You are the same yesterday, today and forever more.

2. Father, in the name of Jesus, I am sorry for all my sins,
    I repent of my pride, iniquities, and wickedness. Also,
    I ask for your mercy, in Jesus' name.

3. Let healing flow into my life, flow into my home, city,
    nation, and the world over. LORD, wipe off from
    me every manifestation of the prison life. I refuse
    to manifest the life of a prisoner, in Jesus Name
    (Zechariah 9:11).

4. LORD, you are the perfection of beauty, infuse your
    beauty into every area of my life. Where beauty has
    faded, add color to my life and make my life bright
    again, in Jesus' name (Psalms 50:2).

5. Father, keep me from all forms of afflictions from
    now on, in Jesus' name (1 Chronicles 4:10).

6. Father, terminate every attack on my life that has made
    me formless or that has not allowed my true image to
    be reflected, in Jesus' name. Let your light shine in
    every area of my life, Father.

7. LORD, because I am your child, no unbeliever around
    me will outshine me, in Jesus' name. I shall be found
    to be ten times better than the best of those around
    me, in SING: you are the Lord that healeth me; you
    are the LORD my healer; you sent your Word and
    healed my disease; you are the LORD my healer.

Day 19

Taking It by Force

"And from the days of John the Baptist until now the kingdom of heaven suffereth violence, and the violent take it by force."
(Matthew 11:12)

As it was while Christ and His disciples walked the earth, the same is true today – the Kingdom of God is by power and righteousness. The Kingdom is to be the primary focus of the believer; it operates by power principles. Failure to understand these principles makes one's destined end and dreams a mirage.

The enemy is a violent and bitter adversary and must be stopped by proactive, defensive force. Whatever the LORD Jesus Christ offers at Calvary for the redeemed is only enforced and delivered on the platform of warfare. You must know what belongs to you so that you may apply the relevant force for delivery (Matthew 11:11-15). Until you fight the good fight of faith, the delivery of eternal life and all other redemptive benefits are not in view (1 Timothy 6:12). Contention, for what is rightfully ours, is the principle behind the recovery and delivery of life's inheritance (Deuteronomy 2:24).

According to Isaiah 53:12, the spoils of life are shared among the strong. The weak do not share in the spoils of life. Victory in spiritual warfare is what qualifies a man for sharing in the spoils of life (1 Samuel 30:18-20; 2 Chronicles 20:25). It is people that share the spoils of life that take their place among the great in life. Those who cannot share in the spoils of life remain small, little, irrelevant and insignificant and exploited. It takes strength in life to do exploits (Daniel 11:32, Isaiah 53:12). Strength is conventionally the main determinant of victory (Luke 11:21-22).

In 2 Corinthians 10:3-4, we are made to understand that, *"For though we walk in the flesh, we do not war after the flesh: (For the weapons of our warfare are not carnal, but mighty through God to the pulling down of strong holds)."* The day a child is born, he begins a lifetime of battle. Everyone living is engaged in one form of battle or the other. Many have become prisoners of war (POWs) brutally abused and despicably treated by captors. Deliverance is by force because the enemy does not release his captives easily or willingly.

PRAYER POINTS

Pray this way:

1. Father, for every battle I must fight in life, let me come out a victor and not a victim in Jesus' name (1 Corinthians 15:57).

2. Every power working, in the order of the Prince of Persia, to hijack my blessings, be arrested in Jesus' name (Daniel 10:12-21).

3. Father, as I fight the battles of life, equip me with the right weapons to ensure victory in Jesus' name.

4. Father GOD, I dispatch your fire to the heavenly realm to destroy every power working against my life, family, success, and prosperity, in Jesus' name.

5. Father, set me free from the hand of my captors, spiritual or human, in Jesus' name (Psalms 79:11).

6. I break every curse designed to get me close to my life goals but never complete achievement in my job, ministry, marriage, family and business in Jesus' name.

7. LORD Jesus, wipe every manifestation of imprisonment off my life. I refuse to live my life as a prisoner, in Jesus' name (Zechariah 9:11).

8. Father, send your angels to battle on my behalf. Please cause every good and virtue in me that the devil has imprisoned to be released to me, in Jesus' name (Daniel 10:11-13).

9. Let every arrow of shame and reproach backfire, in the Name of Jesus.

10. Father, help me not to spend my life only laboring daily to make money. Please bring me to the point where my money will, in turn, work for me in Jesus' name (Ecclesiastes 10:19).

Day 20

DWELLING IN THE SECRET PLACE

"He that dwelleth in the secret place of the Most High shall abide under the shadow of the Almighty" (Psalm 91:1).

To understand the phrase, "He that dwells in the secret place of the Most High," you must look at its composite parts individually. In Hebrew, 'Most High' is the word 'El-yon', meaning "the Supreme One," "the Owner of heaven and earth," and "the God who is over and above all things that are." The secret place of the Most High is a hint of where God wants every believer to be. If we can understand what this means, we will be a long way toward the fire and purity of revival. In order that we might understand the secret place better, the LORD Jesus came to reveal to us the mystery and unlock the door. He says, *"Abide in Me, and I will abide in you"* (John 15:4).

It does not take a very brilliant person to make the connection between Psalms 91 and John 15. The language is the same. Read John 15, then go back and read Psalms 91 again. All those words – abide, dwell, live – they all mean the same thing. "He who dwells in the secret place of the Most High shall abide under the shadow of the Almighty" goes right together with "Abide in Me, and I will abide in you."

That secret place is literally one of physical safety and security, but access to it is conditional. This gives us the most intense illustration of the very essence of personal relationship. Man has no innate, inbuilt shelter. Alone, he stands without shelter against the elements and must run to the ultimate shelter himself. In verse 1, God is offering us more than protection; it is as if He rolls out the hospitality mat and personally invites us in. However, He also lists the conditions we must meet before mentioning the promises included in His part of the bargain. That's because our part must come first. To abide in the shadow of the Almighty, we must have first chosen to dwell in the shelter of the Most High.

PRAYER POINTS

Bless God's majesty, His holy name – Jehovah Shalom, Jehovah Elohim, All knowing, Powerful, Sufficient, The Monarch of the Universe, Ancient of Days, Rock of Ages, etc. Simply worship Him.

Ask the LORD to draw you closer and let you hear, see and obey Him. Pray that your soul will indeed pant after the LORD (Psalms 42:1-2).

Now declare:

1. Holy Spirit, please sustain me in the place of closeness to you that I may continue to enjoy the bounty of heaven. LORD Jesus, please shield me from every

power that causes a leak of blessings from my life, in Jesus' name.

2. Father, please send your fire to destroy every altar erected against my ability to continually preach the Good News, in Jesus' name (Acts 23:12).

3. LORD, as I dwell in your secret place, I pray that no unbeliever around me will outshine me, in Jesus' name. I shall be found to be better than the best of them around me, in Jesus' name (Daniel 1:19-20).

4. Father, as I dwell in your secret place, let my ears be opened to the voice of your Spirit, in Jesus' name (Revelations 2:29).

5. Holy Spirit, please shield my eyes away from things that will misinform my heart, in Jesus' name (2 Samuel 12:21-23)!

6. Thank you, Holy Spirit, for answered prayers, in Jesus' name!

Day 21

EAGLE BELIEVERS SOARING

As an eagle stirs up its nest, Hovers over its young, Spreading out its wings, taking them up, Carrying them on its wings, So the LORD alone led him, And there was no foreign god with him.
(Deuteronomy 32:11-12)

In the text above, it is amazing to see so many wonderful references about the eagle. Mountains, rivers, storms, clouds, and the rain pose no problem for the eagle because it has strong wings. No wonder the LORD spoke so much about the eagle in the Bible, probably more than any other bird known to man. No wonder He called you an eagle, the king of all birds.

In addition, reading through these passages of Scripture, one can see that it is the Grace of God that saves Israel and saves us as believers in our present day walk with the LORD. Salvation, then and now is by the grace of God alone! This is evident in Exodus 19:4, where God reminded the nation of Israel about their rescue from slavery by His great strength and brought them to Himself. Very important. It was not their strength, intellect, connections or military might that liberated them. No! As God rescued the Israelites from 430 years of slavery in Egypt, so He desires to rescue us out of our sin into eternal life with Him. If we will turn away from our sinful lives and ask Him to save us, He will do so.

We Are Eagles By Redemption:

- Redeemed to Walk in Dominion: Genesis 1:28; Numbers 23:23; Isaiah 8:8.

- Ordained to Be Salt of The Earth and Light of The World: Matthew 5:6; Obadiah 1:21.

- We Are Redeemed as Kings to Reign on Earth: Revelation 5:9-10.

- We Are Redeemed to Be Fruitful, Not Barren: Psalms 128:1-5; Isaiah 5:1-13; Psalms 1:3.

- We Are Redeemed to Be Greater Than All Old Testament Saints: Matthew 11:11.

- We Are to Manifest Seven Redemptive Treasures: Revelation 5:12 says:"...Lamb that was slain to receive power, and riches, and wisdom, and strength, and honor, and glory, and blessing."

- We Are Supernatural Beings: Psalms 82:6.

PRAYER POINTS

Declare:

1. Father, let the world see your greatness, power, glory and mighty acts in my life in Jesus' name. *"Ye have seen..."* (Exodus 19:4) Father, as eagles bear their young away from danger; deliver me from danger, enslavement and bondage.

2. Father, as eagles soar upon the current of winds, let me overcome every restriction to my progress in Jesus' name.

3. Father, as eagles overcome the power of storms, I overcome every storm on the path of my destiny, by a mighty act of God, in Jesus' name.

4. Father, as eagles bear her young ones and protect them from danger in her nest:

    • I command divine protection over my life, in Jesus' name.

    • I command divine provision over my life, in Jesus' name.

    • I command angelic care over my life, in Jesus' name.

5. Father, in the order of deliverance from Egypt, I receive redemption from calamity, sorrow and disappointment.

6. Father, let me soar high like an eagle.

ABOUT THE AUTHOR

Pastor (Dr.) Fadel, as the author is fondly called, is the Special Assistant to the General Overseer and Chairman, the Redeemed Christian Church of God (RCCG), North America Operations. He trained as a mechanical engineer, and later obtained a master's degree in Operations Research from Wayne State University in 1990. In addition, he earned an MBA from the Lawrence Technological University, also in Michigan, in 1993. His most recent academic degree is a Doctor of Ministry in Transformational Leadership from Bakke Graduate University, Seattle, WA.

He was mentored by the General Overseer of The Redeemed Christian Church of God (RCCG) Worldwide, Pastor E.A. Adeboye, who later commissioned Fadel for the work he is doing now. However, it started from Fadel pioneering a house fellowship in his basement in 1991, which later became the first RCCG parish in North America. Under his leadership to date, RCCG, North America Operations has grown to 924 parishes in 132 zones, 40 provinces, and 11 regions over the expanse of North and Central America. Each year, thousands attend the annual RCCG, North America Operations convention at the campground in Floyd, Texas of over 700 acres.

Pastor Fadel also works tirelessly to develop other national programs to enable RCCG, North America Operations ministers and workers to grow into maturity in their Christian walk and service. By the grace of God, he is happily married to Pastor Manita, a medical doctor specializing in pediatric medicine, and they are blessed with three children.

NOTES

NOTES

NOTES

NOTES

www.ingramcontent.com/pod-product-compliance
Lightning Source LLC
Chambersburg PA
CBHW071624040426
42452CB00009B/1477